Real Estate Market Cycles

Navigating the Ups and Downs of Property Investment

While every precaution has been taken in the preparation of this book, the publisher assumes no responsibility for errors or omissions, or for damages resulting from the use of the information contained herein.

REAL ESTATE MARKET CYCLES

First edition. December 4, 2023.

ISBN: 979-8223112792

Written by Andan Maharma.

Table of Contents

Adnan Maharma

Chapter 1: Introduction to Market Cycles: The Ebb and Flow of Real Estate

The world of real estate is a dynamic and ever-changing landscape. Just like the tides of the ocean, the real estate market experiences distinct patterns of rise and fall, growth, and contraction. In this chapter, we'll dive into the fundamental concepts of market cycles and explore how they shape the realm of property investment.

Understanding the Ebb and Flow:

Market cycles are the heartbeat of the real estate industry. They are the rhythmic patterns of expansion and contraction that influence property values, demand, and investor sentiment. From the peaks of exuberant growth to the troughs of economic turmoil, these cycles are a natural part of the economic ecosystem.

The Nature of Market Cycles:

Market cycles are often driven by a complex interplay of economic factors, government policies, population trends, and technological advancements. As investors, understanding the nature of these cycles is crucial for making informed decisions and managing risks effectively.

The Four Phases of a Market Cycle:

Market cycles can be broadly categorized into four distinct phases:

- Expansion: The phase of growth and optimism, where property values rise, demand surges, and opportunities abound.

- Peak: The zenith of the market, characterized by high prices, intense competition, and increased speculative activity.

- Contraction: The period of decline and uncertainty, marked by falling property values and a decrease in demand.

- Trough: The bottom of the cycle, where prices stabilize or start to rebound, offering opportunities for astute investors.

Riding the Wave: Navigating Market Cycles:
As an investor, understanding these phases and their impact on the real estate landscape is akin to learning to navigate the open sea. Each phase presents unique challenges and opportunities, requiring a strategic approach and a keen awareness of market dynamics.

Market cycles are a constant dance that shapes the ebb and flow of the real estate world. By grasping the fundamental principles behind these cycles, you'll be better equipped to make informed investment decisions, ride the waves of opportunity, and ultimately thrive in the ever-changing realm of property investment.

In the next chapter, we'll delve into the invaluable lessons offered by the historical perspective of past market cycles, allowing us to learn from the successes and failures of those who came before us.

Chapter 2: The Historical Perspective: Lessons from Past Market Cycles

In the vast tapestry of real estate, the threads of history weave a compelling narrative of triumphs and tribulations. Past market cycles stand as a testament to the cyclical nature of the industry and offer invaluable insights for today's investors. In this chapter, we embark on a journey through time, uncovering the stories and lessons of those who navigated the tumultuous waters of real estate market cycles.

Learning from the Past: A Glimpse into the Cycles of Yesteryears

The annals of history hold a treasure trove of stories that shed light on the ebb and flow of real estate market cycles. Consider the Roaring Twenties, a time of unprecedented economic prosperity and skyrocketing property values. Investors reveled in the abundance of opportunity, confident that the good times would never end. However, the crash of 1929 brought this exuberance to a screeching halt, ushering in the Great Depression and a period of unparalleled economic turmoil. The lessons learned from this era underscore the importance of prudence and a long-term perspective, as well as the need to remain vigilant against the dangers of unchecked speculation.

Case Study: The Great Recession and Its Lessons

One of the most prominent chapters in recent real estate history is the Great Recession of 2007-2009. The housing bubble, fueled by risky lending practices and the belief that property values would perpetually climb, ultimately burst with catastrophic consequences. As home prices plummeted, countless homeowners found themselves underwater on their mortgages, and the financial system teetered on the brink of collapse. This crisis highlighted the critical importance of responsible lending, risk assessment, and regulatory oversight. The scars left by the Great Recession continue to shape real estate practices today, serving as a stark reminder of the potential consequences of unchecked market exuberance.

Wisdom from the Veterans: Voices from the Past

The stories of seasoned investors who weathered past market cycles offer invaluable insights. Take, for example, the experiences of those who navigated the challenging landscape of the 1980s, a period marked by high inflation and interest rates. These individuals learned the art of adapting to shifting conditions, embracing innovative financing strategies, and seizing opportunities amid adversity. Their journeys serve as a beacon of inspiration for modern investors, highlighting the resilience required to thrive in even the most tumultuous of times.

Applying Historical Lessons Today: Navigating the Modern Era

Drawing parallels between historical market cycles and the present day provides a strategic advantage. By identifying recurring patterns and recognizing the warning signs of potential downturns, investors can make informed decisions and position themselves for success. The lessons of history underscore the importance of diversification, careful risk management, and a commitment to continuous learning in navigating the ever-evolving landscape of real estate.

The history of real estate market cycles is a tapestry interwoven with the threads of triumph and hardship, innovation and adaptation. The lessons gleaned from the past offer a roadmap for modern investors, guiding them through the intricacies of market dynamics. By immersing ourselves in the stories of those who faced the challenges of yesteryears, we gain a deeper appreciation for the cyclical nature of the industry and the enduring principles that anchor us amidst the shifting tides.

In the upcoming chapter, we will delve into the world of economic indicators, exploring how these metrics serve as compasses, guiding us through the complex terrain of real estate market cycles.

Chapter 3: Economic Indicators and Their Impact on Real Estate Trends

In the intricate dance of real estate market cycles, economic indicators serve as the choreographers, guiding the movements of property values, demand, and investor sentiment. This chapter delves into the world of economic indicators, unveiling their significance and exploring how they shape the intricate tapestry of real estate trends.

Understanding Economic Indicators: The Pulse of the Economy

Economic indicators are the vital signs of an economy, revealing its health and vitality. Think of them as a physician's toolkit used to diagnose the current state of economic affairs. These indicators encompass a wide array of metrics that measure different aspects of economic activity. From the performance of the labor market to the fluctuations in consumer spending, each indicator offers a unique perspective on the economic landscape.

Unraveling the Web of Influence: How Indicators Impact Real Estate

The intricate interplay between economic indicators and real estate trends is akin to a delicate ecosystem, where changes in one realm have cascading effects on another. For instance, consider the relationship between the unemployment rate and housing demand. When unemployment is low, more individuals have stable incomes, making them more likely to pursue homeownership. This increased demand can contribute to rising property values.

Similarly, interest rates are a powerful force in the realm of real estate. As the cost of borrowing money fluctuates, it directly affects the affordability of homes. When interest rates are low, borrowing costs decrease, making it more enticing for individuals to invest in real estate. Conversely, higher interest rates can cool demand and lead to more cautious investment behaviors.

Key Economic Indicators that Influence Real Estate:

Gross Domestic Product (GDP): GDP is the total value of all goods and services produced within a country. A growing GDP often translates to higher consumer confidence, increased job creation, and a stronger housing market. Conversely, a stagnating GDP may lead to diminished consumer spending and housing demand.

Unemployment Rate: The unemployment rate reflects the percentage of the labor force that is jobless and actively seeking employment. Low unemployment rates often indicate a robust job market, which contributes to higher disposable income and greater demand for homes.

Consumer Confidence Index: This index measures consumer sentiment and expectations regarding economic conditions. High consumer confidence can lead to increased spending on big-ticket items, such as homes. Conversely, low consumer confidence may lead to more cautious spending and lower demand for real estate.

Interest Rates: Central banks control interest rates, influencing the cost of borrowing money. Lower interest rates make mortgages more affordable, encouraging homebuying and investment. Higher interest rates can have the opposite effect, potentially dampening demand.

Inflation Rate: Inflation refers to the general increase in prices over time. Moderate inflation can indicate a healthy economy, but rapid inflation can erode purchasing power and impact affordability.

Housing Starts: Housing starts indicate the number of new residential construction projects initiated. High housing starts suggest a growing demand for housing, while low starts may indicate a slowing market.

Case Study: The Subprime Mortgage Crisis and Economic Indicators

The cataclysmic subprime mortgage crisis of 2008 stands as a stark reminder of the interconnectedness between economic indicators and real estate trends. The proliferation of subprime mortgages, coupled with lax lending standards, led to a housing bubble. Economic indicators such as rising foreclosure rates and declining consumer confidence served as early warning signs, foreshadowing the impending crisis.

Strategically Navigating Economic Indicator Trends:

In the realm of real estate investment, the ability to interpret and respond to economic indicators is a powerful asset. During periods of robust economic growth and low unemployment, investors might consider focusing on residential properties, anticipating increased demand. Conversely, during economic uncertainty, a shift towards rental properties may offer stability.

Economic indicators serve as a compass, guiding investors through the labyrinth of real estate market cycles. By mastering the language of these indicators, investors can decipher the intricate patterns of the market, anticipate shifts, and position themselves for success. In the subsequent chapter, we will delve into the first phase of the real estate market cycle: expansion.

Chapter 4: Expansion: Riding the Wave of Opportunity

In the grand symphony of real estate market cycles, the phase of expansion is like a crescendo of optimism and growth. Investors, developers, and homeowners alike revel in the rising tide of property values, demand surges, and the promise of lucrative opportunities. This chapter delves into the exhilarating journey of riding the wave of expansion and navigating the complexities of this dynamic phase.

The Prelude: Setting the Stage for Expansion

The stage for the expansion phase is carefully set as a harmonious interplay of economic indicators. These indicators collectively create an environment of economic growth, stability, and increasing consumer confidence. As the curtain rises on the expansion phase, investors can anticipate the following key dynamics:

Rising Demand: Job creation is in full swing, and consumer confidence soars. This leads to a surge in demand for housing, both for homeownership and rental properties. The market becomes a bustling hub of activity as potential buyers and tenants seek suitable accommodations.

Increasing Property Values: The confluence of strong demand and limited housing supply results in a rapid escalation of property values. Investors find themselves witnessing appreciation in real estate holdings at a remarkable pace, creating opportunities for substantial capital gains.

Development and Construction: The expansion phase ushers in a boom in construction and development. Builders and developers seize the opportunity to capitalize on the heightened demand for new homes, commercial spaces, and infrastructure projects.

Strategies for Success in Expansion:

Strategic Acquisition: Investors can strategically acquire properties that exhibit potential for significant appreciation. In-depth market research and analysis help identify neighborhoods with strong growth indicators and upcoming development plans.

Value-Add Investments: Renovating or upgrading properties can further enhance their market value. Investors may opt to improve existing structures, introduce modern amenities, or optimize property layouts to attract higher rents or sale prices.

Equity Building: As property values continue to climb, investors are presented with a unique opportunity to build equity rapidly. This increased equity can be leveraged to expand their real estate portfolio, secure favorable financing terms, or explore new investment avenues.

Mitigating Risks and Challenges:

Overconfidence: The exhilaration of expansion can lead to overconfidence and potentially hasty investment decisions. It is imperative for investors to remain grounded, adhere to sound investment principles, and conduct thorough due diligence before making acquisition choices.

Market Saturation: The surge in demand during expansion can sometimes lead to market saturation, where an oversupply of properties exceeds the demand. Investors need to carefully monitor supply and demand dynamics to avoid potential pitfalls associated with a saturated market.

Interest Rate Shifts: Although interest rates may remain relatively favorable during the expansion phase, sudden shifts in monetary policy can impact borrowing costs and affordability. Investors should remain attuned to potential changes and their potential consequences.

The Crescendo and Beyond: Maximizing Opportunities

As the expansion phase reaches its crescendo, investors find themselves at the precipice of opportunity. This phase represents a strategic window to make impactful decisions that align with both prevailing market trends and individual investment goals. Maximizing profits during this phase demands a delicate equilibrium of astute decision-making, rigorous risk management, and a perceptive eye for emerging trends.

The expansion phase is akin to a thrilling ascent, characterized by a crescendo of opportunities and potential rewards. By harnessing the predictive power of economic indicators, seizing strategic acquisitions, and capitalizing on value-enhancing endeavors, investors position themselves to skillfully ride the wave of expansion. As we prepare to ascend to the next chapter, the summit of the market cycle beckons: the peak phase, where the promise of high rewards converges with the ever-present specter of increased risks.

Chapter 5: Peak: Maximizing Profits and Managing Risks

In the grand theater of real estate market cycles, the peak phase stands as a moment of heightened anticipation and calculated risk. As property values reach their zenith and the market teeters on the edge of change, investors must navigate a delicate balance between seizing maximum profits and safeguarding against the impending descent. This chapter delves into the intricate art of managing opportunities and risks during the peak phase.

The Apex of the Journey: Reaching the Market's Zenith

The peak phase is the apex of the market's journey, where the culmination of factors gives rise to a market at its most vibrant and prosperous state. During this exhilarating phase, investors experience:

Maximized Profits: Property values have ascended to their highest point, promising substantial capital gains for investors who entered the market earlier. Those who made strategic acquisitions during the expansion phase are now reaping the rewards of their foresight and savvy decision-making.

Intense Competition: The allure of potentially substantial profits creates a frenzy of activity in the market. Buyers, including seasoned investors and newcomers alike, compete fervently for a limited inventory of properties.

Speculative Activity: The peak phase may see a surge in speculative behavior, as investors attempt to capitalize on the momentum of rising property values. This can sometimes lead to market imbalances and unsustainable growth.

Strategies for Profiting and Managing Risks at the Peak:

Tactical Selling: Savvy investors who recognize the peak phase may opt to strategically sell properties to capitalize on the peak of property values. This approach allows investors to lock in gains and protect against potential downturns.

Portfolio Diversification: Diversifying one's investment portfolio beyond real estate can provide a cushion against potential market fluctuations. Exploring other asset classes or geographic markets can mitigate risk.

Due Diligence: Diligence in research and analysis becomes paramount during the peak phase. Scrutinizing potential acquisitions, thoroughly evaluating market fundamentals, and assessing growth potential are crucial to avoid overpaying based on market hype.

Navigating the Perilous Precipice: Risks and Challenges

Market Correction: The euphoria of the peak phase is often followed by a market correction or downturn. Investors must be prepared for the possibility of declining property values, reduced demand, and a shift in market sentiment.

Overleveraging: In the pursuit of maximizing profits, some investors may overextend themselves by taking on excessive debt or leveraging their investments. This approach can leave investors vulnerable to financial strain in a downturn.

Speculative Traps: The allure of quick profits may tempt investors into speculative ventures that lack sustainable long-term potential. Focusing on investments grounded in solid fundamentals is crucial to avoid speculative pitfalls

The Descent: Preparing for the Inevitable

As the peak phase gradually transitions into the next phase, prudent investors take proactive steps to navigate the impending changes:

Profit Preservation: As property values start to plateau, investors shift their focus toward preserving profits. This may involve evaluating exit strategies, deciding whether to sell or hold properties, and diversifying investment holdings.

Risk Mitigation: Preparing for potential market shifts involves reducing exposure to high-risk investments, revisiting financing arrangements to ensure sustainability, and maintaining sufficient cash reserves to weather potential storms.

The peak phase embodies the pinnacle of real estate market cycles, where maximized profits and calculated risk-taking converge. By leveraging strategic selling, diversifying portfolios, and maintaining rigorous due diligence, investors can capitalize on the opportunities presented by the peak phase while proactively managing potential risks. As we descend from this summit, the next phase of the market cycle beckons: contraction, a time of introspection, adaptation, and the search for opportunities amidst uncertainty.

Chapter 6: Contraction: Surviving the Downturn and Identifying Opportunities

In the symphony of real estate market cycles, the contraction phase is a period of introspection and adaptation. As the market takes a downward turn from the peak, investors must navigate the challenges of reduced demand and declining property values. Yet, within this season of change lies the potential for astute investors to identify hidden opportunities and emerge even stronger. This chapter delves into the art of weathering the storm of contraction while strategically seeking out avenues for growth.

The Dawn of Contraction: Navigating the Descent

The contraction phase follows the exuberance of the peak, marked by a shift in market dynamics. Investors encounter:

Reduced Demand and Softened Activity: As the market corrects itself, demand for real estate softens. Potential buyers become more cautious, and sellers may experience longer listing periods. Transaction volumes decrease, signaling a period of adjustment.

Declining Property Values: The euphoria of the peak gives way to declining property values. Investors who failed to exit during the peak may now grapple with diminishing profits or potential losses.

Market Correction and Balanced Sentiment: The speculative frenzy of the peak subsides, leading to a more balanced market sentiment. Investors reassess their strategies as they navigate the evolving landscape.

Strategies for Thriving in Contraction:

Strategic Selling and Capital Preservation: Investors with a keen sense of market timing may opt to sell certain properties before values decline further. Preserving capital enables them to be nimble and take advantage of future opportunities.

Cash Reserves and Liquidity: Maintaining ample cash reserves becomes paramount during contraction. Liquidity provides the flexibility to weather the storm, cover operational expenses, and seize distressed assets at favorable prices.

Targeted Acquisitions and Value Enhancement: Contraction often reveals distressed properties or assets with untapped potential. Investors can strategically acquire such properties at discounted prices and embark on value-enhancing projects to position them for future growth.

Uncovering Opportunities Amidst Uncertainty:

Distressed Properties and Renovation Projects: Contraction unveils distressed properties that may present opportunities for value-add investments. Renovations and repositioning can transform these properties, making them attractive for the eventual recovery phase.

Market Research and Emerging Trends: Diligent market research during contraction uncovers emerging trends and areas with growth potential. Identifying underserved markets or asset classes can lead to well-timed and strategic investments.

Creative Financing and Negotiation: Contraction can prompt lenders to adapt their financing terms. Investors who explore creative financing solutions and negotiate effectively can secure more favorable terms for their acquisitions.

Navigating Challenges and Mitigating Risks:

Liquidity Management and Financial Stability: Maintaining adequate liquidity is essential for managing financial obligations and seizing opportunities during the contraction phase. This may involve refinancing loans or securing credit lines.

Mitigating Property Vacancies and Management: Reduced demand can lead to increased vacancies. Implementing effective property management strategies, tenant retention initiatives, and flexible leasing terms can help mitigate the impact.

Patience and Long-Term Perspective: Contraction is a phase of recalibration. Patience and a long-term perspective are essential as investors weather the storm and position themselves for the eventual recovery phase.

The Contraction's Legacy: Preparing for the Rebound

As the contraction phase unfolds, investors prepare for the eventual rebound and the dawn of a new cycle:

Strategic Holdings and Stewardship: Investors may choose to hold well-performing assets during contraction, positioning them for potential appreciation during the recovery phase.

Opportunistic Investments and Timing: Contraction unveils opportunities that were obscured during the peak. Investors who strategically deploy capital can capitalize on undervalued assets and emerging trends.

The contraction phase, though marked by challenges, is a period of resilience and adaptability. By adeptly managing financial resources, strategically acquiring distressed assets, and embracing a patient outlook, investors can position themselves to weather the downturn and emerge with renewed strength. As we move forward, the upcoming chapter will delve into the phase of trough, exploring strategies to navigate the depths of market cycles and set the stage for eventual recovery and growth.

Chapter 7: Trough: Strategies for Bottom-Fishing and Recovery

In the intricate symphony of real estate market cycles, the trough phase is a period of both challenge and opportunity. As the market reaches its nadir, investors are presented with the potential to engage in strategic "bottom-fishing," seeking out undervalued assets with the anticipation of future recovery. This chapter delves into the art of navigating the trough, employing savvy strategies to capitalize on the depths of the market cycle and set the stage for resurgence.

Descending into the Trough: Navigating Uncertainty

The trough phase follows the contraction, characterized by a market at its lowest ebb. During this phase, investors confront a confluence of factors:

Depressed Property Values: Property values hit their nadir as demand remains subdued and economic uncertainties persist. The decline in values offers investors the opportunity to acquire properties that were previously out of reach due to inflated prices during the peak phase.

Limited Investment Activity: Market activity and transaction volumes remain subdued as investor confidence wavers. A general sense of caution pervades the investment landscape, leading to a significant slowdown in acquisitions and property transactions.

Potential Distressed Opportunities: The trough often reveals distressed assets and opportunities for value acquisition. Properties facing financial distress, foreclosures, or those that were overlooked during the peak phase become more accessible, opening avenues for creative investment strategies.

Strategies for Bottom-Fishing and Setting the Stage for Recovery:

Strategic Asset Acquisition: Investors engage in strategic asset acquisition, meticulously selecting undervalued properties that hold the potential to appreciate once market conditions improve. Rigorous research and analysis guide the selection of properties with strong fundamentals, such as desirable location, future growth prospects, and alignment with emerging market trends.

Distressed Asset Opportunities: The trough is a prime time for acquiring distressed assets, such as foreclosures or properties facing financial challenges. Investors can capitalize on these opportunities by acquiring properties at significantly discounted prices and implementing value-added improvements to enhance their appeal and marketability.

Patient Capital Deployment: During the trough, investors adopt a patient approach to capital deployment. Recognizing that the full extent of market recovery may take time, investments are made with a focus on long-term potential and future appreciation rather than seeking immediate gains.

Identifying the Turning Point and Positioning for Recovery:

Researching Market Indicators: Investors closely monitor leading indicators that signal the potential for recovery. Positive shifts in economic indicators, employment trends, and consumer sentiment serve as harbingers of the turning point. This information informs strategic decisions on property acquisitions and upgrades.

Selective Property Upgrades: Strategic property upgrades and renovations are undertaken during the trough to enhance value and prepare for the eventual uptick in demand. Investors invest in enhancements that align with anticipated market preferences, positioning properties for greater appeal once recovery takes hold.

Positioning for the Uptrend: As signs of recovery emerge, investors position themselves to capitalize on the impending uptrend. This may involve acquiring additional properties in strategic locations or asset classes expected to experience early revitalization. Investors keenly observe emerging markets and demographic shifts that could drive future demand.

Mitigating Risks and Seizing Recovery:

Risk Assessment and Management: Thorough due diligence is paramount during the trough phase. Investors assess risks, market fundamentals, and potential challenges associated with distressed assets meticulously. Collaboration with real estate professionals and experts aids in making informed investment decisions.

Sufficient Liquidity: Maintaining adequate liquidity during the trough enables investors to seize opportunities as they arise and navigate potential challenges. Liquidity provides the flexibility to act swiftly and decisively when favorable investment prospects present themselves.

Adaptive Strategies: The trough demands adaptive strategies that align with the evolving market landscape. Flexibility and the ability to pivot investment approaches are key to seizing recovery opportunities. Investors adjust their portfolio mix, shift resources, and adapt their investment goals based on changing market dynamics.

The Resilient Rise: Preparing for Renewed Growth

As the trough phase gradually transitions into the next cycle, investors prepare for renewed growth and the promise of a market upswing:

Property Value Appreciation: Investors anticipate property value appreciation as demand gradually strengthens. Holdings positioned for recovery begin to yield positive returns, contributing to enhanced portfolio performance and bolstering investor confidence.

Strategic Dispositions: As the market recovers, investors may consider strategically divesting certain assets that have appreciated during the trough. By capitalizing on increased property values, investors can reallocate resources for future opportunities, optimize their investment portfolios, and further position themselves for growth.

The trough phase is a period of patient positioning and calculated opportunity-seeking. By employing strategic asset acquisition, recognizing distressed asset potential, and patiently awaiting market recovery, investors can lay the groundwork for future growth. The journey through the trough sets the stage for the next chapter, where we will explore the strategies investors can employ to harness the momentum of renewal and embark on a new cycle of expansion and prosperity.

Chapter 8: The Art of Market Analysis: Tools and Techniques

In the dynamic world of real estate investment, the ability to analyze and interpret market trends is a fundamental skill that distinguishes successful investors from the rest. This chapter delves into the art of market analysis, providing insights into the tools and techniques that empower investors to make informed decisions, navigate changing market conditions, and harness the pulse of real estate cycles.

The Foundation of Strategic Decision-Making: Market Analysis

Market analysis is the bedrock upon which real estate investment strategies are built. It involves a systematic examination of key factors that influence property values, demand, and supply dynamics. Investors leverage market analysis to identify opportunities, mitigate risks, and tailor their actions to the prevailing market environment.

Key Metrics for Tracking Market Trends:

Supply and Demand Dynamics: Assessing the balance between supply and demand in a specific market helps investors gauge the potential for property appreciation or depreciation. A thorough understanding of demographic trends, population growth, and employment prospects contributes to accurate demand projections.

Comparable Sales (Comps): Analyzing recent comparable property sales provides insights into prevailing market prices and helps investors determine fair market value. Comps allow investors to identify trends, patterns, and potential outliers that influence their investment decisions.

Price-to-Rent Ratio: This ratio helps investors assess whether it is more cost-effective to buy or rent a property in a particular market. A higher ratio suggests buying might be advantageous, while a lower ratio indicates renting may be more viable.

The Role of Government Policies in Shaping Cycles:

Interest Rates and Monetary Policy: Government policies related to interest rates impact borrowing costs and affordability. Lower rates stimulate demand and property appreciation, while higher rates can dampen demand and lead to stagnation.

Tax Incentives and Regulations: Tax incentives, such as deductions for mortgage interest or property taxes, can influence buyer behavior and demand. Government regulations, such as zoning laws or rent control measures, also shape investment opportunities and market dynamics.

Economic Stimulus and Infrastructure Projects: Government investments in infrastructure projects can enhance property values in specific regions. Improvements in transportation, utilities, and public amenities can attract businesses and residents, driving demand for real estate.

Tools and Techniques for Effective Analysis:

Market Segmentation: Dividing a market into distinct segments, such as residential, commercial, or industrial, allows investors to target specific niches with tailored strategies. Each segment responds differently to market cycles, requiring customized approaches.

SWOT Analysis (Strengths, Weaknesses, Opportunities, Threats): This strategic framework helps investors assess the internal and external factors that influence a property's potential. It aids in identifying opportunities to capitalize on strengths and mitigate weaknesses.

Regression Analysis: This statistical technique identifies relationships between variables, enabling investors to predict future trends based on historical data. Regression analysis helps quantify the impact of different factors on property values.

The Art of Predicting Market Trends:

Technical Analysis: Investors use technical analysis to study historical price and volume patterns, identifying trends and potential turning points. Chart patterns and indicators offer insights into future price movements.

Fundamental Analysis: Similar to stock market analysis, fundamental analysis involves assessing the intrinsic value of a property based on income potential, expenses, and market conditions. This approach guides investment decisions by comparing property values to potential income streams.

Market Sentiment and Consumer Confidence: Gauging market sentiment through surveys, media reports, and consumer confidence indices provides insights into the psychological factors that drive market behavior. Shifts in sentiment can signal changes in demand and market direction.

Mastering the art of market analysis equips investors with a powerful toolkit to navigate the complexities of real estate cycles. By harnessing key metrics, understanding government policies, and employing a range of analytical tools, investors can make well-informed decisions that align with market trends. As we move forward, the following chapters will explore successful strategies tailored to each phase of the real estate market cycle, building on the foundation of market analysis to guide investors toward prosperous outcomes.

Chapter 9: Key Metrics for Tracking Market Trends

In the realm of real estate investment, understanding and effectively analyzing market trends is a cornerstone of success. This chapter delves into the essential metrics that serve as windows into the dynamics of real estate markets. By mastering these metrics, investors can make informed decisions, seize opportunities, and navigate the ebbs and flows of property investment with confidence.

Supply and Demand Dynamics: The Heartbeat of the Market

Housing Starts and Building Permits: These metrics offer a glimpse into the supply side of the market. Housing starts indicate the number of new residential construction projects initiated, reflecting potential future supply. Similarly, building permits represent the permissions granted for new construction. Increasing numbers in these metrics suggest a growing supply of properties, potentially influencing the balance between supply and demand.

Population Growth and Migration Patterns: The local population and migration patterns have a direct impact on demand for housing. Rising population numbers or significant inward migration can lead to increased demand for housing and rental properties. Investors analyze demographic trends to predict shifts in demand and potential investment opportunities.

Inventory Levels: Monitoring inventory levels, or the number of properties available for sale, sheds light on supply levels in the market. High inventory levels may signal a buyer's market, where buyers have more negotiating power due to the abundance of options. Conversely, low inventory levels could indicate a seller's market, potentially leading to rising prices due to increased competition among buyers.

Price and Value Indicators: Unveiling Market Sentiments

Median and Average Sale Prices: These metrics reflect the prices at which properties are being sold in a given market. Observing trends in median and average sale prices over time helps investors identify market sentiment. Rising prices suggest a strong market where demand outpaces supply, while declining prices may indicate a shift in market dynamics.

Price-to-Income Ratio: The price-to-income ratio compares the median home price to the median household income. A higher ratio may indicate that properties are becoming overpriced relative to income levels, potentially leading to affordability challenges for buyers.

Price-to-Rent Ratio: This ratio compares property prices to rental income. A higher ratio may suggest that buying a property is relatively more expensive than renting, potentially leading to increased rental demand. Conversely, a lower ratio may indicate that buying is more financially advantageous.

Market Liquidity and Activity: A Pulse on Investor Engagement

Days on Market (DOM): DOM measures the average number of days a property remains listed before being sold. Shorter DOM values suggest a strong seller's market, where properties are selling quickly due to high demand. Longer DOM values may indicate a buyer's market, potentially providing buyers with negotiation opportunities.

Absorption Rate: The absorption rate reflects how quickly available properties are being sold. A high absorption rate indicates robust demand and a potentially competitive market. Conversely, a low absorption rate may signify weaker demand and a less competitive market.

Sales Volume: Tracking the number of property sales over time provides insights into market activity. Increasing sales volume suggests growing investor interest and confidence in the market's potential.

Economic Context: Beyond Real Estate Borders

Gross Domestic Product (GDP) Growth: GDP growth reflects the overall health of the economy. Positive GDP growth indicates economic expansion, which can contribute to increased consumer spending and demand for housing.

Employment Trends and Unemployment Rates: The job market is closely tied to housing demand. A strong job market with low unemployment rates often leads to increased demand for housing as individuals seek stable housing options.

Consumer Confidence Index: This index measures consumer sentiment and their outlook on the economy. Optimistic consumer sentiment can drive higher consumer spending, potentially leading to increased demand for housing.

Putting Metrics to Work: Informed Decision-Making

Market Analysis: Integrating and analyzing these metrics provides a comprehensive view of market conditions. By considering how these metrics interact and influence each other, investors can gain insights into market trends and make data-driven investment decisions.

Timing Strategies: Metrics like DOM and absorption rates can help investors time their entry into markets. A high DOM might present opportunities for negotiation, while a low absorption rate may indicate a competitive market where quick decisions are crucial.

Risk Assessment: Metrics such as price-to-rent ratios and unemployment rates aid in assessing risk. High price-to-rent ratios may indicate potential overvaluation, while rising unemployment rates could signal potential economic challenges affecting the market.

Understanding and utilizing these key metrics empowers investors to navigate real estate market dynamics with precision. By leveraging these insights, investors can make informed choices, optimize their investment strategies, and position themselves for success. As we progress, the upcoming chapters will delve into specialized strategies for each phase of the real estate market cycle, all built upon the foundation of market analysis.

Chapter 10: The Role of Government Policies in Shaping Cycles

Government policies wield a significant influence over the ebbs and flows of the real estate market, shaping its direction and impacting investor strategies. This chapter delves into the intricate interplay between government policies and the real estate market, exploring how regulations, incentives, and fiscal decisions can drive market cycles and guide investor behavior.

Interest Rates and Monetary Policy: The Financial Pulse

Interest Rate Movements: Central banks control interest rates, which directly affect borrowing costs. Lower interest rates can stimulate borrowing and investment, leading to increased demand for real estate. Conversely, higher rates can dampen demand, leading to potential market contraction.

Quantitative Easing (QE): Central banks may implement QE, which involves purchasing government bonds or assets to inject liquidity into the economy. This can lead to lower mortgage rates and increased investor appetite for real estate.

Taxation and Incentives: Shaping Buyer Behavior

Mortgage Interest Deductions: Government policies that allow mortgage interest deductions can incentivize homeownership by reducing the after-tax cost of borrowing. This can drive demand for properties, particularly in markets with favorable tax policies.

Property Tax Policies: Varied property tax rates and exemptions influence real estate affordability and investor decisions. Lower property taxes may attract investors and residents to certain markets, while high taxes can dampen demand.

First-Time Homebuyer Incentives: Government programs that offer financial assistance or tax incentives to first-time homebuyers can stimulate demand in specific market segments and support property sales.

Regulations and Zoning Laws: Shaping Supply and Demand

Land Use and Zoning: Government zoning laws dictate how land can be used, affecting property values and potential uses. Zoning changes can impact property demand, development opportunities, and property values.

Rent Control: Government-enforced rent control policies limit the amount landlords can charge for rent. While they can provide affordability for tenants, they may impact investor returns and influence investment decisions.

Environmental Regulations: Regulations related to environmental protection can impact property development and influence investor decisions in markets focused on sustainable and green development.

Economic Stimulus and Infrastructure Investment: A Catalyst for Growth

Infrastructure Projects: Government investments in transportation, utilities, and public amenities can enhance property values in specific regions. Improved infrastructure can attract businesses and residents, driving demand for real estate.

Economic Stimulus Packages: During economic downturns, governments may implement stimulus measures that inject funds into the economy. These measures can boost consumer spending, support job creation, and indirectly impact the real estate market.

Global Factors and Trade Policies: Beyond Borders

Foreign Investment Policies: Government regulations on foreign investment can influence demand for properties from international buyers. Changes in these policies can impact market dynamics and property prices.

Trade Agreements: Trade policies and agreements can influence economic growth and job creation, indirectly impacting the demand for real estate in markets tied to specific industries.

Navigating the Government's Impact: Investor Strategies

Policy Analysis: Staying informed about government policies and their potential impacts is crucial for investors. Understanding how policy changes can influence supply, demand, and property values allows investors to make proactive decisions.

Adaptive Strategies: Government policies can shift market dynamics. Investors should remain flexible and adjust their strategies in response to policy changes, seeking opportunities and mitigating risks.

Diversification: A diversified portfolio can help investors manage risk posed by policy shifts. By investing across different markets and asset types, investors can reduce their exposure to specific policy-driven challenges.

Government policies are a powerful force in shaping the real estate market's trajectory. The push and pull of policy decisions can lead to cycles of growth and contraction. By understanding the nuances of government policies and their potential impacts, investors can navigate market cycles with agility and seize opportunities that arise from shifting policy landscapes. In the chapters ahead, we'll explore strategies tailored to each phase of the real estate market cycle, building upon the understanding of government policies to guide investors toward success.

Chapter 11: Thriving in Expansion: Finding Gems in a Booming Market

The expansion phase of the real estate market cycle is a period of optimism, growth, and opportunity. As property values rise and demand surges, investors can capitalize on favorable conditions to maximize returns. This chapter delves into strategies that empower investors to thrive during expansion, identifying lucrative investment opportunities and making informed decisions to harness the full potential of a booming market.

Understanding the Expansion Phase: A Time of Growth

Rising Demand and Property Values: During expansion, increased consumer confidence and economic growth drive demand for real estate. This demand, coupled with limited supply, results in rising property values and potential appreciation.

Low Vacancy Rates: As demand for properties increases, vacancy rates tend to decline. Investors witness strong occupancy rates and may even experience rental rate growth.

Economic Growth and Job Creation: Robust economic indicators, including GDP growth and low unemployment rates, contribute to a thriving market environment. Job creation supports housing demand and rental growth.

Strategies for Thriving in Expansion:

Strategic Property Selection: Identify emerging neighborhoods and areas with growth potential. Conduct thorough research to understand local demographics, infrastructure developments, and amenities that attract residents and tenants.

Value-Add Renovations: Upgrade properties to meet current market demands and preferences. Renovations that enhance curb appeal, energy efficiency, and modern amenities can attract higher rents and premium tenants.

Portfolio Optimization: Reevaluate your investment portfolio during expansion. Consider reallocating resources to properties that align with current market trends and have the potential for higher appreciation.

Capitalizing on Appreciation: During expansion, property values tend to rise. Consider refinancing properties to access equity for new investments or to fund value-added upgrades.

Adapting Lease Structures: Adjust lease terms to capture potential rent increases. Incorporate rent escalations or periodic reviews to ensure rental income keeps pace with market trends.

Mitigating Risks and Planning for the Future:

Scenario Analysis: Anticipate potential market corrections and assess the impact on your portfolio. Conduct scenario analysis to evaluate how different market conditions could affect your investments.

Maintaining Cash Reserves: While expansion offers lucrative opportunities, it's important to maintain sufficient cash reserves for unexpected market shifts or investment needs.

Investment Diversification: Diversify your portfolio across property types and geographic locations. This strategy helps reduce risk and exposure to localized market fluctuations.

Monitoring Market Indicators: Continuously track market trends and indicators. Being proactive in identifying shifts in demand or potential oversaturation helps you make timely decisions.

Thriving in the expansion phase requires a combination of strategic thinking, thorough analysis, and adaptability. By capitalizing on rising property values, strategic renovations, and smart portfolio optimization, investors can seize opportunities to maximize returns. As we delve deeper into the upcoming chapters, we'll explore strategies tailored to each phase of the real estate market cycle, building upon the foundation of expansion to guide investors toward continued success.

Chapter 12: Peak Performance: Selling High and Protecting Investments

The peak phase of the real estate market cycle is characterized by soaring property values and robust demand. As optimism prevails, investors have the opportunity to capitalize on the high point of the cycle by selling properties for substantial profits and safeguarding their investments. This chapter explores strategies to achieve peak performance during this phase, focusing on optimal selling tactics and risk management to navigate the eventual transition.

Understanding the Peak Phase: Reaching New Heights

Peak Property Values: The peak phase represents the pinnacle of property values within the market cycle. Economic growth, low interest rates, and high demand converge to drive property prices to their highest point. Investors benefit from substantial appreciation in property values during this phase.

Intense Investor Activity: Peak phases attract heightened investor activity. As news of rising property values spreads, investors scramble to capitalize on the favorable conditions, often resulting in increased competition for properties.

Potential Oversaturation: While demand is strong, the market may become susceptible to oversaturation. Speculative buying can lead to an influx of properties on the market, potentially leading to a slowdown or even a decline in prices.

Strategies for Peak Performance:

Strategic Property Sales: During the peak phase, consider selling properties that have experienced significant appreciation. Capitalize on the higher property values by divesting assets that have reached their peak, allowing you to lock in profits.

Portfolio Optimization: Evaluate your portfolio and consider divesting underperforming or overvalued properties. Reallocate resources to properties with strong growth potential or those that align with evolving market trends.

Timing the Market: While predicting exact market peaks is challenging, being attuned to market indicators and trends can help you recognize signals of potential plateau or decline. This awareness enables you to make informed decisions about property sales.

Tax Planning: Collaborate with tax professionals to develop tax-efficient strategies. Options may include utilizing 1031 exchanges to defer capital gains taxes or implementing other tactics to minimize tax liabilities.

Risk Mitigation: Diversification remains essential even during the peak phase. Spread your investments across different property types and geographic locations to mitigate the impact of localized market downturns.

Protecting Investments and Preparing for Transition:

Capital Preservation: As property values peak, consider reallocating excess funds to more conservative investments. This approach helps protect your capital from potential market fluctuations and downturns.

Cash Reserves: Maintaining sufficient cash reserves is vital to cover ongoing expenses and unexpected challenges. Having readily available liquidity safeguards your financial position.

Reinvestment Strategy: Strategically allocate profits from property sales toward investments with growth potential or those aligned with future market trends. This approach maximizes the use of funds generated from property sales.

Due Diligence: Thoroughly vet any new investment opportunities, especially during the peak phase. Ensure that potential investments align with your long-term goals, risk tolerance, and are supported by comprehensive research.

Transition Planning and Positioning for the Next Phase:

Market Analysis: Continuously monitor market indicators to anticipate potential shifts. A deep understanding of market dynamics equips you to transition smoothly into the next phase of the cycle.

Flexibility in Strategies: Prepare for the possibility of market corrections by maintaining flexibility in your investment strategies. Being adaptable allows you to pivot and capitalize on evolving market conditions.

Education and Knowledge: Stay well-informed about economic trends, government policies, and industry developments. This knowledge empowers you to make informed decisions as you prepare for potential market shifts.

The peak phase is a pivotal time for investors to capitalize on high property values and robust demand. By strategically selling properties, optimizing your portfolio, and safeguarding your investments, you position yourself to navigate potential market shifts with resilience and foresight. As we progress, the upcoming chapters will delve into strategies customized for each phase of the real estate market cycle, building upon the principles of peak performance to guide investors toward continued success.

Chapter 13: Navigating Contraction: Adapting and Staying Afloat

The contraction phase of the real estate market cycle presents unique challenges and opportunities for investors. As property values stabilize or decline and demand softens, prudent strategies are essential to weather the downturn and position yourself for recovery. This chapter delves into effective tactics to navigate the contraction phase, focusing on adaptability, risk mitigation, and strategic decision-making to ensure your investments remain resilient.

Understanding the Contraction Phase: Adjusting to Change

Stabilizing Property Values: The contraction phase marks a period of stability or decline in property values. Factors such as reduced demand, economic uncertainties, and changing market sentiment contribute to this stabilization.

Rising Vacancy Rates: As demand softens, vacancy rates tend to increase. With fewer tenants or buyers in the market, property owners may face challenges in maintaining occupancy levels and rental income.

Economic Challenges: Economic indicators may signal a slowdown or recession, impacting the overall health of the economy. Job growth may stagnate, consumer spending could decrease, and investor confidence may waver.

Strategies for Navigating Contraction:

Property Repositioning: Adapt to shifting demand by repositioning properties. This could involve making renovations or improvements to enhance property appeal and attract tenants or buyers in a more competitive market.

Cash Flow Management: Prioritize maintaining positive cash flow by scrutinizing expenses and optimizing property management practices. A well-managed cash flow is vital to weathering the challenges of the contraction phase.

Flexible Rental Terms: Offer flexible rental terms, such as short-term leases or rent concessions, to entice tenants and maintain occupancy levels during a time of reduced demand.

Value Preservation: Preserve property value by promptly addressing maintenance and repair needs. Well-maintained properties retain their appeal to potential tenants or buyers.

Risk Mitigation and Protecting Investments:

Loan Refinancing: Explore the possibility of refinancing loans to secure more favorable terms, lower interest rates, or extended repayment schedules. This can alleviate financial pressure during challenging times.

Cash Reserves: Strengthen cash reserves to provide a safety net in case of unexpected expenses or revenue shortfalls. Having adequate liquidity helps manage financial uncertainties.

Diversification Review: Reevaluate your portfolio diversification strategy to ensure it minimizes exposure to specific risks associated with the contraction phase.

Property Disposition: Assess the potential benefits of selling underperforming assets or properties with limited growth potential. Reallocation of resources from such properties can strengthen your overall portfolio.

Positioning for Recovery and Future Opportunities:

Market Analysis: Continuously monitor market indicators and trends to identify early signs of recovery. This positions you to take advantage of opportunities as the market begins to rebound.

Network Building: Build and nurture relationships with fellow investors, real estate professionals, and service providers. Networking can provide valuable insights and potential collaboration opportunities.

Research and Education: Stay informed about market conditions, economic trends, and potential policy changes that could impact the real estate market. Knowledge empowers you to make well-informed decisions.

Navigating the contraction phase requires resilience, adaptability, and strategic planning. By repositioning properties, managing cash flow, mitigating risks, and positioning for recovery, you can successfully navigate the challenges and uncertainties of the contraction phase. As we proceed, the upcoming chapters will delve into strategies customized for each phase of the real estate market cycle, building upon the principles of contraction navigation to guide investors toward continued success.

Chapter 14: Rising from the Trough: Turning Adversity into Advantage

The trough phase of the real estate market cycle marks a period of transition from contraction to expansion. While challenges may persist, this phase presents unique opportunities for savvy investors to position themselves for future growth. This chapter explores strategies to rise from the trough, leveraging market shifts and transforming adversity into advantage through strategic decision-making, value identification, and forward-thinking approaches.

Understanding the Trough Phase: Transitioning Toward Recovery

Recovery Signs: The trough phase indicates the initial stages of market recovery. Signs of stabilizing property values and renewed investor interest become apparent.

Gradual Demand Increase: Demand for properties begins to recover from the contraction phase, albeit at a slower pace. This gradual resurgence sets the stage for potential expansion.

Economic Revival: Economic indicators may start to improve, reflecting a shift toward growth. Job creation and consumer spending contribute to the market's upward trajectory.

Strategies for Turning Adversity into Advantage:

Value Acquisition: Identify undervalued properties that have the potential for appreciation as the market rebounds. Acquiring such properties positions you for substantial future gains.

Distressed Asset Opportunities: Consider distressed or foreclosed properties that can be acquired at a discount. These assets may present significant value upon successful repositioning.

Long-Term Vision: Adopt a long-term investment perspective. Properties acquired during the trough phase can yield impressive returns as the market continues to recover.

Strategic Partnerships: Collaborate with other investors or real estate professionals to pool resources, share insights, and jointly capitalize on emerging opportunities.

Risk Mitigation and Seizing Future Growth:

Thorough Due Diligence: Conduct comprehensive research before making investment decisions. Thorough due diligence minimizes risks associated with property selection and acquisition.

Financial Readiness: Strengthen your financial position by maintaining cash reserves and optimizing your investment structure. This prepares you to capitalize on value-driven opportunities.

Adaptive Strategies: Remain flexible and open to adjusting your strategies as market conditions evolve. Agility allows you to respond effectively to changing dynamics.

Positioning for Expansion and Maximizing Potential:

Market Analysis: Continuously monitor market trends to gauge the trajectory of the recovery phase. Being well-informed positions you to take advantage of expansion opportunities.

Strategic Property Upgrades: Enhance property value by making targeted improvements that align with market preferences and emerging trends.

Networking and Market Insights: Cultivate relationships with industry experts, local stakeholders, and other investors. Networking provides access to valuable market insights and potential collaboration.

Rising from the trough requires a combination of foresight, strategic decision-making, and a willingness to capitalize on emerging opportunities. By identifying undervalued properties, leveraging distressed asset opportunities, and maintaining a long-term vision, you position yourself to turn adversity into advantage.

Chapter 15: Investors' Tales: Triumphs and Tribulations Across Cycles

The real estate market is a landscape of triumphs and tribulations, shaped by the diverse experiences of investors who navigate its cycles. This chapter delves into the stories of real-life investors who have weathered various market phases, sharing their successes, challenges, and the valuable lessons they've learned. Through these tales, readers gain insights into the strategies, decisions, and mindsets that have contributed to investors' triumphs and their ability to overcome tribulations.

Triumphs in Expansion: Learning from Success

Investor Success Stories: Explore narratives of investors who strategically capitalized on the expansion phase. Discover how they identified emerging markets, optimized property portfolios, and leveraged growth opportunities.

Maximizing Profits: Learn from investors who timed property sales during peak phases, realizing substantial profits by selling high and positioning themselves for future success.

Value-Add Strategies: Dive into tales of investors who implemented value-add renovations and enhancements to attract tenants, drive rental income, and enhance property value.

Tribulations in Contraction: Navigating Challenges

Adaptation During Contraction: Explore the experiences of investors who faced property value declines and rising vacancy rates during the contraction phase. Understand how they adapted their strategies to maintain resilience.

Cash Flow Management: Learn from investors who navigated cash flow challenges and implemented innovative approaches to manage expenses and preserve financial stability.

Risk Mitigation: Delve into stories of investors who weathered economic uncertainties by diversifying their portfolios and making strategic property dispositions.

Triumphs and Lessons in Recovery: Bouncing Back Stronger

Recovery Strategies: Discover how investors seized opportunities during the recovery phase, identifying undervalued properties, forming strategic partnerships, and positioning themselves for growth.

Strategic Property Acquisitions: Learn from successful investors who capitalized on distressed assets and turned them into lucrative opportunities as the market rebounded.

Long-Term Vision: Gain insights from investors who embraced a long-term perspective, reaping the rewards of their patient and strategic investments made during the trough phase.

Navigating Through All Cycles: Key Takeaways and Insights

Adaptability and Flexibility: Understand the importance of adapting investment strategies to the changing dynamics of each market cycle, showcasing the resilience of successful investors.

Risk Management: Learn how prudent risk management, including diversification and financial preparedness, has helped investors weather challenges and capitalize on opportunities.

Market Insights: Discover the power of staying informed about market trends, economic indicators, and government policies, which has allowed investors to make informed decisions across cycles.

Investors' tales serve as powerful testimonies to the dynamic nature of the real estate market. By learning from the experiences of those who have triumphed and overcome tribulations, readers gain valuable insights into effective strategies, adaptable mindsets, and the enduring wisdom that guides successful investors. As we proceed to the final chapters, we'll continue to build upon these insights, exploring future trends and the evolving landscape of real estate to guide investors toward continued success.

Chapter 16: Case Study: Weathering the Storm - The Great Recession and Its Lessons

Setting the Stage: The Great Recession Unveiled

Origins of the Crisis: The Great Recession was triggered by a complex interplay of factors, including the housing bubble, subprime mortgage crisis, and excessive risk-taking in financial markets. The chapter delves into the root causes of the crisis, providing a comprehensive understanding of its origins.

Impact on Real Estate: The housing market collapse had far-reaching effects on real estate. Property values plummeted, foreclosure rates soared, and banks tightened lending standards, making it challenging for investors to secure financing. Readers gain insight into the extent of the impact on the real estate sector and its ripple effects.

Investor Strategies Amidst Crisis: Navigating Turbulent Waters

Adapting to Market Shifts: The case study profiles investors who adjusted their strategies to navigate the crisis. They shifted from speculative purchases to a focus on value-driven acquisitions, recognizing the need to adapt to changing market dynamics.

Risk Mitigation: The chapter explores how investors mitigated risks during the crisis. Diversification emerged as a key strategy, with investors spreading their investments across different property types and geographic locations. Disposing of underperforming assets and strengthening cash reserves were also critical risk management tactics.

Innovative Financing: Readers gain insights into the creative financing solutions that investors employed to secure funding amidst the credit crunch. From private lenders to seller financing, investors leveraged unconventional approaches to continue their operations.

Lessons Learned: Wisdom Forged in Adversity

Long-Term Vision: Investors who weathered the storm exhibited a long-term perspective. They resisted making panic-driven decisions and instead focused on their investment goals, recognizing that market cycles are a natural part of the real estate landscape.

Resilience and Adaptability: The case study showcases how resilient investors were in the face of adversity. They adjusted their strategies, embraced new opportunities, and demonstrated adaptability, illustrating the importance of resilience during challenging times.

Thorough Due Diligence: The chapter highlights the emphasis on due diligence. Investors meticulously researched distressed assets, analyzed market trends, and conducted comprehensive property evaluations before making investment decisions.

Recovery and Growth: Emerging Stronger

Positioning for Recovery: Readers learn how investors identified early signs of recovery and strategically positioned themselves to capitalize on the rebounding market. Those who remained vigilant and attuned to market indicators were able to seize opportunities as the market began to recover.

Value-Centric Approach: The case study delves into investors who adopted a value-centric approach, acquiring undervalued properties during the trough phase. As the market rebounded, these properties saw significant appreciation, underscoring the power of value-driven investments.

The case study of the Great Recession serves as a testament to the resilience, adaptability, and innovative thinking of real estate investors. By exploring their experiences, strategies, and lessons, readers gain a comprehensive understanding of how investors weathered one of the most significant market crises in history. These lessons continue to guide investors forward as they navigate the evolving landscape of real estate investment, incorporating these insights into their strategies for continued success.

Chapter 17: Innovators and Visionaries: Pioneers Who Thrived in Challenging Times

Throughout history, the real estate market has been shaped by innovators and visionaries who demonstrated extraordinary foresight and adaptability during challenging periods. This chapter shines a spotlight on these pioneers, exploring their remarkable stories and the groundbreaking strategies that allowed them to thrive in the face of adversity. By delving into their achievements, readers gain insights into the transformative power of innovation, creativity, and forward-thinking approaches.

The Early Pioneers: Shaping the Landscape

Innovative Development: Discover the stories of visionaries who transformed barren landscapes into thriving communities through innovative development and infrastructure projects. These pioneers laid the foundation for successful urban planning and property development.

Adaptive Reuse: Explore the creative minds behind adaptive reuse projects, who repurposed historic buildings and structures, breathing new life into forgotten spaces and revitalizing entire neighborhoods.

Innovations During Economic Downturns: Lessons in Resilience

Contrarian Investing: Learn from investors who defied conventional wisdom by making bold acquisitions during economic downturns. Discover how these contrarian approaches paid off as markets eventually rebounded.

Technology Adoption: Delve into the stories of innovators who harnessed emerging technologies during challenging times. From digital marketing to virtual tours, these pioneers transformed the way properties were marketed and sold.

Green Innovators: Sustainability Amidst Adversity

Sustainable Development: Explore how forward-thinking developers integrated sustainable practices into their projects, even when economic conditions were challenging. Their commitment to sustainability set new standards for environmentally conscious real estate.

Renewable Energy Integration: Discover the pioneers who incorporated renewable energy solutions into their properties, showcasing how sustainability initiatives can lead to long-term cost savings and market differentiation.

Entrepreneurial Spirit: Navigating Regulatory Challenges

Navigating Regulation: Learn from entrepreneurs who navigated complex regulatory landscapes to bring innovative real estate concepts to life. Their perseverance and ability to work within legal frameworks paved the way for new market segments.

The stories of innovators and visionaries who thrived in challenging times serve as beacons of inspiration for today's real estate investors. By exploring their achievements, readers gain insights into the power of creative thinking, adaptability, and a willingness to embrace change. As we move forward to the final chapters, we'll continue to build upon these lessons and explore the role of technology, sustainability, and continuous learning in shaping the future of real estate investment.

Chapter 18: Technology's Role in Shaping Future Cycles

In the rapidly evolving landscape of real estate, technology has emerged as a transformative force, reshaping how properties are bought, sold, managed, and experienced. This chapter delves into the profound impact of technology on future real estate cycles, exploring how innovative solutions, data-driven insights, and digital platforms are revolutionizing the industry. By examining the role of technology, readers gain a glimpse into the exciting possibilities that lie ahead and the strategies to harness its potential.

The Digital Revolution: Transforming the Real Estate Landscape

Proptech Evolution: Delve into the emergence of proptech, where startups and established players alike are leveraging technology to streamline transactions, enhance property management, and create immersive experiences for stakeholders.

Blockchain and Smart Contracts: Explore how blockchain technology and smart contracts are revolutionizing property transactions by enhancing security, transparency, and efficiency in real estate deals.

Data-Driven Insights: Shaping Investment Strategies

Predictive Analytics: Discover how data analytics and predictive modeling are empowering investors to make informed decisions, predict market trends, and strategize for future cycles.

Market Transparency: Learn how technology is fostering greater market transparency, enabling investors to access real-time data, property histories, and market analyses, thereby reducing uncertainty and improving decision-making.

Digital Marketing and Experience Enhancement: The Future of Engagement

Virtual and Augmented Reality: Explore the role of virtual and augmented reality in property marketing and visualization, providing potential buyers and investors with immersive experiences.

Digital Advertising and Marketing: Understand how digital advertising and marketing are reshaping how properties are promoted, reaching wider audiences and enhancing market reach.

Smart Cities and Sustainable Innovation: Paving the Way Forward

Smart City Integration: Delve into the concept of smart cities, where technology is integrated into urban planning, infrastructure, and property development, resulting in enhanced living experiences and sustainable communities.

Green Innovations: Discover how technology is advancing sustainability in real estate, with innovations in energy-efficient buildings, smart appliances, and renewable energy integration.

Redefining Property Management and Operations: Efficiency and Automation

Smart Building Management: Explore how Internet of Things (IoT) technology is revolutionizing property management by enabling remote monitoring, predictive maintenance, and energy optimization.

Automated Workflows: Learn how automation is streamlining property operations, from rent collection and maintenance requests to lease renewals and financial reporting.

Technology's transformative influence on real estate is undeniable, and its impact on future market cycles promises to be profound. By embracing technological advancements, real estate investors can leverage data-driven insights, optimize processes, and create enhanced experiences for stakeholders. As we conclude our exploration of technology's role in shaping the future of real estate investment, we'll continue to build upon these insights and examine the evolving landscape of sustainable practices and the enduring cycle of wisdom in the world of real estate.

Chapter 19: The Evolving Landscape of Real Estate: Green Trends and Sustainability

In an era of heightened environmental awareness and the pressing need for sustainable practices, the real estate industry is undergoing a profound transformation. This chapter explores the evolving landscape of green trends and sustainability in real estate, examining how eco-friendly practices, energy efficiency, and environmentally conscious development are reshaping the way properties are designed, built, managed, and valued. By delving into these trends, readers gain insights into the future of sustainable real estate and its implications for investors.

The Green Revolution: A Paradigm Shift in Real Estate

Sustainable Development: Discover how sustainable building practices, such as energy-efficient designs, low-carbon materials, and green construction techniques, are redefining the way properties are developed.

Environmental Certifications: Explore the significance of certifications like LEED (Leadership in Energy and Environmental Design) and other eco-friendly labels that quantify a property's sustainability and environmental impact.

Energy Efficiency and Smart Technologies: A Sustainable Future

Energy-Efficient Design: Learn how energy-efficient features, such as smart thermostats, LED lighting, and insulation technologies, are reducing carbon footprints and operational costs for property owners.

Renewable Energy Integration: Discover how solar panels, wind turbines, and other renewable energy sources are being integrated into property designs to generate clean energy and reduce reliance on traditional power sources.

Resilient and Adaptive Design: Future-Proofing Properties

Climate-Resilient Construction: Understand how properties are being designed and built to withstand the challenges of climate change, including extreme weather events, rising sea levels, and other environmental risks.

Adaptive Reuse for Sustainability: Explore how adaptive reuse projects repurpose existing structures, minimizing environmental impact and contributing to sustainable urban development.

Eco-Friendly Operations and Maintenance: Long-Term Sustainability

Green Property Management: Learn how property managers are implementing eco-friendly practices, from waste reduction and efficient landscaping to water conservation and sustainable tenant amenities.

Circular Economy Principles: Discover the concept of a circular economy, where materials are reused, recycled, or repurposed, reducing waste and promoting sustainable resource management.

Investment Implications and Market Demand: Green Real Estate

Eco-Conscious Investors: Explore the growing demand for green real estate among environmentally conscious investors, who seek properties that align with their values and offer long-term sustainability.

Financial Benefits: Understand how green properties can yield financial benefits, including reduced operational costs, enhanced tenant attraction and retention, and potential government incentives.

The evolution of green trends and sustainability in real estate represents a transformative shift with far-reaching implications. By embracing eco-friendly practices, energy efficiency, and environmentally conscious development, investors have the opportunity to not only contribute to a more sustainable future but also reap the rewards of enhanced property value and market demand. As we conclude our exploration of the evolving landscape of real estate, the final chapter will delve into the cycle of wisdom, encapsulating the enduring principles that guide successful investors across all market phases.

of wisdom, encapsulating the enduring principles that guide successful investors across all market phases.

Chapter 20: The Cycle of Wisdom: Continuously Adapting and Learning in Real Estate

At the heart of successful real estate investment lies a timeless principle—the cycle of wisdom. This chapter explores the profound concept of continuously adapting and learning in the dynamic world of real estate. Drawing from the collective experiences of seasoned investors, this chapter encapsulates the enduring strategies, mindset, and values that guide investors through all market phases. By understanding the cycle of wisdom, readers gain insights into the essential traits that foster resilience, growth, and enduring success.

Embracing Lifelong Learning: The Foundation of Wisdom

Curiosity and Exploration: Discover how an insatiable thirst for knowledge drives investors to explore new trends, emerging technologies, and evolving market dynamics to make informed decisions.

Continuous Education: Learn how successful investors prioritize ongoing education, attending workshops, seminars, and courses to stay abreast of industry developments and enhance their expertise.

Adapting to Change: Navigating the Cycles

Flexibility and Agility: Understand the importance of remaining flexible in investment strategies, adapting to changing market conditions, and embracing innovative approaches to meet evolving demands.

Resilience Through Downturns: Explore how a resilient mindset helps investors navigate challenging downturns with composure, seeing them as opportunities for growth rather than setbacks.

Strategic Decision-Making: Informed and Thoughtful

Thorough Due Diligence: Delve into the critical role of due diligence in making informed investment decisions, from market research and property analysis to risk assessment and financial modeling.

Analytical Thinking: Learn how analytical thinking allows investors to dissect complex situations, evaluate potential risks and rewards, and make calculated decisions based on data-driven insights.

Building Relationships and Networks: Collaborative Wisdom

Networking and Collaboration: Understand how cultivating relationships with fellow investors, real estate professionals, and industry experts creates a network of shared knowledge, insights, and potential partnerships.

Mentorship and Guidance: Explore the transformative impact of mentorship, where seasoned investors provide guidance, wisdom, and practical advice to those navigating the real estate journey.

Fostering Ethical Practices: The Bedrock of Wisdom

Integrity and Transparency: Learn how ethical conduct, transparency, and integrity form the foundation of long-lasting relationships and contribute to a positive reputation in the industry.

Sustainable and Responsible Investing: Discover the significance of investing with a long-term perspective, considering the impact on communities, environments, and stakeholders for sustainable growth.

The cycle of wisdom serves as a compass, guiding investors through the ever-changing landscape of real estate. By embracing lifelong learning, adapting to change, making strategic decisions, building relationships, and fostering ethical practices, investors embody the principles that underpin lasting success. As we conclude our journey through the chapters, readers are invited to reflect on these essential traits and integrate them into their own real estate endeavors, embarking on a path of continuous growth, resilience, and wisdom.

The journey through the chapters of "Real Estate Market Cycles: Navigating the Ups and Downs of Property Investment" has been a comprehensive exploration of the intricate world of real estate. From understanding the historical context and economic indicators to thriving in different market phases and embracing innovation, each chapter has provided valuable insights into the strategies, mindsets, and principles that guide successful investors.

In the realm of real estate, knowledge is indeed power. By delving into the foundations of market cycles, learning from historical lessons, and analyzing economic indicators, investors can make informed decisions that drive success in every phase. The expansion phase presents opportunities for growth, the peak phase demands strategic profit maximization, the contraction phase requires adaptability, and the trough phase is a realm of potential value creation.

Investors have the chance to leverage market analysis tools, understand government policies, and learn from the triumphs and tribulations of those who have walked the path before. The role of technology, sustainability, and continuous learning is transforming the real estate landscape, allowing investors to embrace innovation and adapt to changing market dynamics.

Above all, the cycle of wisdom serves as an enduring guidepost. By continuously adapting, learning, and growing, investors can navigate the complexities of the real estate market with resilience and strategic acumen. The principles of integrity, ethical conduct, and a long-term perspective ensure that success is not only measured in financial gains but also in contributing positively to communities and environments.

As you embark on your own real estate journey, remember that each chapter in this book is a stepping stone toward mastery. Embrace the lessons, strategies, and stories shared within these pages, and weave them into your own unique approach. Whether you're a seasoned investor or a newcomer to the field, the principles explored here will equip you to confidently navigate the ever-changing tides of the real estate market, making wise decisions and reaping the rewards of a well-guided investment journey.